Published in Great Britain by Grange Books PLC
The Grange, Units 1–6 Kingsnorth Industrial Estate,
Hoo, Nr Rochester, Kent ME3 9ND
tel  01634 256000
fax 01634 255500

E-mail  Grange Books@AOL.com

First published in 1999
The collection, text and illustrations,
copyright © Random House Australia Pty Ltd, 1999

ISBN 1840133198

*Head of Department:* Gordon Cheers
*Publisher, Children's and Young Adults' Books:* Linsay Knight
*Publishing Co-ordinator:* Sarah Sherlock
*Managing Editor:* Marie-Louise Taylor
*Art Director:* Stan Lamond
*Designer:* Joy Eckermann
*Cover Design:* Bob Mitchell
*Typesetter:* Dee Rogers

Film separation by Pica Colour Separation Overseas Pte Ltd,
Singapore
Printed in Hong Kong by Dah Hua Printing Press Co., Ltd.

*For permission to reproduce any of the illustrations in this book, please
contact Sarah Sherlock at Random House Australia.*

*Editor*

**ALICE MILLS** is a senior university lecturer in children's literature, fantasy and myth. She has a master's degree in literature from the University of Cambridge. She also holds a graduate diploma in professional psychology, and is particularly interested in Jungian theory about child development and the psychological aspects of literature for children. Alice has edited *The Random House Children's Treasury, The Random House Children's Treasury Gift Set* and *Favourite Bedtime Stories.* Alice has also published many scholarly articles on children's books, fantasy and myth, and has edited a collection of essays titled *Seriously Weird.*

# THERE WAS A YOUNG LADY WHOSE NOSE...
## and other nonsense rhymes

### by Edward Lear

There was an Old Derry down Derry, who loved to see little folks merry;
So he made them a Book, and with laughter they shook
At the fun of that Derry down Derry.

# INTRODUCTION

Edward Lear's nonsense has delighted children for over 150 years. All his life he wanted to gain fame and fortune as a serious artist, but his paintings have been forgotten. He is remembered for the nonsense drawings and verses that he made up to entertain children. Lear never married, never had children of his own, but he knew exactly what would make children laugh.

Perhaps he knew so well how to amuse children because his own childhood was lonely. He was born in 1812 in London, at a time when families tended to be enormous. Edward was the twentieth of twenty-one children. When he was a very small child, life was comfortable for the Lear family, but when he was four, his father Jeremiah lost money and went to jail because he could not pay his debts. Even though Jeremiah was soon released, the family struggled with poverty from then on, and Edward's mother had little time and attention to give to her small son. Lear was ill as well as lonely. He suffered from asthma and bronchitis in the cold wet English winters. At five he developed epilepsy, an illness not well understood in his lifetime, and he was always afraid that people would shrink from him because of his fits.

He tried to earn his living by painting. The big landscape paintings that he worked on for months and years were not very good works of art. He made enough money from art, though, to travel in Europe, India and the Holy Land, finding sunny places to spend the winters in, always dreaming of artistic success, always disappointed.

Success came when he published collections of the nonsense rhymes and pictures he had entertained children with. Lear was shy with adults, but cheerful and happy in children's company, when he met them on his travels, in hotels, or in their parents' stately homes. With his big bushy beard and eyes shining from behind thick glasses, he was an ideal temporary uncle. Years later, when they were grown up, children remembered how he drew, rhymed and sang his nonsense for them.

His nonsense is a world where nothing is too serious. Lear's own life is revealed in some of the limericks. He felt throughout his life that he was painfully different from other people. His poems about odd faces, huge beards, strange chins and remarkably long noses, turn Lear's own worries about his appearance (especially his nose) to cheerful fun. To be different, in these poems, is to have special talents and gifts.

Lear's nonsense offers a feast of amazing and outrageously comical stories, of mishaps and triumphs, oddities and exaggerations. In our world children are asked to grow up and become serious all too soon. Lear invites all his readers, adult and child alike, to share and enjoy a little child's world of play, surprise and wonder.

It is a very similar story for Lewis Carroll, the other master of nonsense, who was born thirty years after Lear. Lear suffered from epileptic fits; Carroll was troubled with a stammer all his life. Both men were at ease in the company of children, rather than adults. Both had an official, public career that was not in the least nonsensical, Lear as artist, Carroll as lecturer in mathematics. Both delighted in entertaining children with their nonsense creations, and both became popular and famous because of their nonsense rather than their work in the adult world.

You might like to follow Lear's example and compose a personalised limerick for a child. Nonsense limericks often begin and end with a place name (There was a young person of —). Fill in the blank, and find a rhyme for the place name. Sydney, for instance, rhymes with "didn't he"; London rhymes with "sundown" or "rundown". Choose an amazing story for the middle of the limerick. You can exaggerate, or make it up. The more outrageous and extraordinary your limerick is, the better it will be.

ALICE MILLS, 1999

*Shown here is a draft of one of Lear's limericks. The final version (below) has an Old Lady, rather than a Young Person, sinking underground.*

There was an Old Lady of Chertsey, who made a remarkable curtsey;
She twirled round and round, till she sank underground,
Which distressed all the people of Chertsey.

There was an Old Person of Dutton, whose head was as small as a button;
So to make it look big, he purchased a wig,
And rapidly rushed about Dutton.

There was an Old Man of the Hague, whose ideas were excessively vague;
He built a balloon to examine the moon,
That deluded Old Man of the Hague.

There was an Old Man in a tree, who was horribly bored by a Bee;
When they said, "Does it buzz?" he replied, "Yes, it does!
It's a regular brute of a Bee!"

There was a Young Lady of Sweden, who went by the slow train to Weedon;
When they cried, "Weedon Station!" she made no observation,
But thought she should go back to Sweden.

There was a Young Lady whose eyes were unique as to colour and size;
When she opened them wide, people all turned aside,
And started away in surprise.

There was a Young Lady of Ryde, whose shoe-strings were seldom untied;
She purchased some clogs, and some small spotty Dogs,
And frequently walked about Ryde.

There was an Old Man of Corfu, who never knew what he should do;
So he rushed up and down, till the sun made him brown,
That bewildered Old Man of Corfu.

There was an Old Man of Apulia, whose conduct was very peculiar;
He fed twenty sons upon nothing but buns,
That whimsical Man of Apulia.

There was a Young Lady whose bonnet came untied when the birds sat upon it;
But she said, "I don't care! all the birds in the air
Are welcome to sit on my bonnet!"

There was an Old Man on a hill, who seldom, if ever, stood still;
He ran up and down in his Grandmother's gown,
Which adorned that Old Man on a hill.

There was an Old Person of Rheims, who was troubled with horrible dreams;
So to keep him awake they fed him with cake,
Which amused that Old Person of Rheims.

There was a Young Lady of Portugal, whose ideas were excessively nautical;
She climbed up a tree to examine the sea,
But declared she would never leave Portugal.

There was an Old Person of Mold, who shrank from sensations of cold;
So he purchased some muffs, some furs, and some fluffs,
And wrapped himself well from the cold.

There was an Old Man of Coblenz, the length of whose legs was immense;
He went with one prance from Turkey to France,
That surprising Old Man of Coblenz.

There was an Old Man of the coast, who placidly sat on a post;
But when it was cold he relinquished his hold,
And called for some hot buttered toast.

There was a Young Person of Smyrna, whose Grandmother threatened to burn her;
But she seized on the Cat, and said, "Granny, burn that!
You incongruous Old Woman of Smyrna!"

There was an Old Man of El Hums, who lived upon nothing but Crumbs;
Which he picked off the ground, with the other birds round,
In the roads and the lanes of El Hums.

There was an Old Man of Peru, who watched his wife making a stew;
But once, by mistake, in a stove she did bake
That unfortunate Man of Peru.

There was a Young Lady of Tyre, who swept the loud chords of a lyre;
At the sound of each sweep she enraptured the deep,
And enchanted the city of Tyre.

There was an Old Man who said, "Hush! I perceive a young bird in this bush!"
When they said, "Is it small?" he replied, "Not at all!
It is four times as big as the bush!"

There was an Old Man of Leghorn, the smallest that ever was born;
But quickly snapt up he was once by a Puppy,
Who devoured that Old Man of Leghorn.

There was an Old Person of Ems who casually fell in the Thames;
And when he was found, they said he was drowned,
That unlucky Old Person of Ems.

There was an Old Person of Spain, who hated all trouble and pain;
So he sat on a chair with his feet in the air,
That umbrageous Old Person of Spain.

There was an Old Man who supposed that the street door was partially closed;
But some very large Rats ate his coats and his hats,
While that futile Old Gentleman dozed.

There was an Old Person of Bar, who passed all her life in a Jar;
Which she painted pea-green, to appear more serene,
That placid Old Person of Bar.

There was an Old Man in a pew, whose waistcoat was spotted with blue;
But he tore it in pieces, to give to his Nieces,
That cheerful Old Man in a pew.

There was an Old Man of the Isles, whose face was pervaded with smiles;
He sang "High dum diddle," and played on the fiddle,
That amiable Man of the Isles.

There was an Old Person of Tring, who embellished his nose with a ring;
He gazed at the moon every evening in June,
That ecstatic Old Person of Tring.

There was an Old Man of Nepaul, from his horse had a terrible fall;
But, though split quite in two, with some very strong glue
They mended that man of Nepaul.

There was an Old Man of Kamschatka, who possessed a remarkably fat Cur;
His gait and his waddle were held as a model
To all the fat dogs in Kamschatka.

There was an Old Man of Kilkenny, who never had more than a penny;
He spent all that money in onions and honey,
That wayward Old Man of Kilkenny.

There was an Old Lady of Prague, whose language was horribly vague;
When they said, "Are these caps?" she answered, "Perhaps!"
That oracular Lady of Prague.

There was an Old Person of Hurst, who drank when he was not athirst;
When they said, "You'll grow fatter!" he answered, "What matter?"
That globular Person of Hurst.

There was an Old Person of Buda, whose conduct grew ruder and ruder,
Till at last with a hammer they silenced his clamour,
By smashing that Person of Buda.

There was an Old Man of the West, who wore a pale plum-coloured vest;
When they said, "Does it fit?" he replied, "Not a bit!"
That uneasy Old Man of the West.

There was an Old Man with a beard, who sat on a Horse when he reared;
But they said, "Never mind! you will fall off behind,
You propitious Old Man with a beard!"

There was an Old Person of Cadiz, who was always polite to all ladies;
But in handing his daughter, he fell into the water,
Which drowned that Old Person of Cadiz.

There was an Old Man of the Cape, who possessed a large Barbary Ape;
Till the Ape, one dark night, set the house all alight,
Which burned that Old Man of the Cape.

There was an Old Person of Bangor, whose face was distorted with anger;
He tore off his boots, and subsisted on roots,
That borascible Person of Bangor.

There was an Old Man of Whitehaven, who danced a quadrille with a Raven;
But they said, "It's absurd to encourage this bird!"
So they smashed that Old Man of Whitehaven.

There was a Young Person of Janina, whose uncle was always a-fanning her;
When he fanned off her head, she smiled sweetly and said,
"You propitious Old Person of Janina!"

There was an Old Man of the Dee, who was sadly annoyed by a Flea;
When he said, "I will scratch it!" they gave him a hatchet,
Which grieved that Old Man of the Dee.

There was an Old Man of Melrose, who walked on the tips of his toes;
But they said, "It ain't pleasant to see you at present,
You stupid Old Man of Melrose."

There was a Young Lady of Lucca, whose lovers completely forsook her;
She ran up a tree, and said "Fiddle-de-dee!"
Which embarrassed the people of Lucca.

There was an Old Man with a gong, who bumped at it all the day long;
But they called out, "Oh law! you're a horrid old bore!"
So they smashed that Old Man with a gong.

There was an Old Lady of Chertsey, who made a remarkable curtsey;
She twirled round and round, till she sank underground,
Which distressed all the people of Chertsey.

There was a Young Lady of Russia, who screamed so that no one could hush her;
Her screams were extreme — no one heard such a scream
As was screamed by that Lady of Russia.

There was an Old Person of Basing, whose presence of mind was amazing;
He purchased a steed, which he rode at full speed,
And escaped from the people of Basing.

There was an Old Person of Cromer, who stood on one leg to read Homer;
When he found he grew stiff, he jumped over the cliff,
Which concluded that Person of Cromer.

There was an Old Man of th' Abruzzi, so blind that he couldn't his foot see;
When they said, "That's your toe," he replied, "Is it so?"
That doubtful Old Man of th' Abruzzi.

There was a Young Lady of Hull, who was chased by a virulent Bull;
But she seized on a spade, and called out, "Who's afraid!"
Which distracted that virulent Bull.

There was an Old Man of the Nile, who sharpened his nails with a file,
Till he cut off his thumbs, and said calmly, "This comes
Of sharpening one's nails with a file!"

There was a Young Lady of Troy, whom several large Flies did annoy;
Some she killed with a thump, some she drowned at the pump,
And some she took with her to Troy.

There was an Old Man of Vienna, who lived upon Tincture of Senna;
When that did not agree, he took Camomile Tea,
That nasty Old Man of Vienna.

There was an Old Man of the South, who had an immoderate mouth;
But in swallowing a dish that was quite full of Fish,
He was choked, that Old Man of the South.

There was an Old Man of the West, who never could get any rest;
So they set him to spin on his nose and his chin,
Which cured that Old Man of the West.

There was an Old Man who said, "How shall I flee from this horrible Cow?
I will sit on this stile, and continue to smile,
Which may soften the heart of that Cow."

There was a Young Lady whose nose was so long that it reached to her toes;
So she hired an Old Lady, whose conduct was steady,
To carry that wonderful nose.

There was an Old Man of Calcutta, who perpetually ate bread and butter;
Till a great bit of muffin, on which he was stuffing,
Choked that horrid Old Man of Calcutta.

There was a Young Lady of Dorking, who bought a large bonnet for walking;
But its colour and size so bedazzled her eyes,
That she very soon went back to Dorking.

There was an Old Person of Rhodes, who strongly objected to toads;
He paid several cousins to catch them by dozens,
That futile Old Person of Rhodes.

There was an Old Person of Anerley, whose conduct was strange and unmannerly;
He rushed down the Strand with a Pig in each hand,
But returned in the evening to Anerley.

There was a Young Lady of Wales, who caught a large Fish without scales;
When she lifted her hook, she exclaimed, "Only look!"
That ecstatic Young Lady of Wales.

There was an Old Man with a poker, who painted his face with red ochre.
When they said, "You're a Guy!" he made no reply,
But knocked them all down with his poker.

There was an Old Man of Vesuvius, who studied the works of Vitruvius;
When the flames burnt his book, to drinking he took,
That morbid Old Man of Vesuvius.

There was an Old Man with an Owl, who continued to bother and howl;
He sat on a rail, and imbibed bitter ale,
Which refreshed that Old Man and his Owl.

71

There was an Old Person of Prague, who was suddenly seized with the plague;
But they gave him some butter, which caused him to mutter,
And cured that Old Person of Prague.

There was an Old Man with a nose, who said, "If you choose to suppose
That my nose is too long, you are certainly wrong!"
That remarkable Man with a nose.

There was a Young Lady of Norway, who casually sat in a doorway;
When the door squeezed her flat, she exclaimed "What of that?"
This courageous Young Lady of Norway.

There was an Old Man of the East, who gave all his children a feast;
But they all ate so much, and their conduct was such,
That it killed that Old Man of the East.

There was an Old Man of Port Grigor, whose actions were noted for vigour;
He stood on his head, till his waistcoat turned red,
That eclectic Old Man of Port Grigor.

There was an Old Person whose habits induced him to feed upon Rabbits;
When he'd eaten eighteen, he turned perfectly green,
Upon which he relinquished those habits.

There was an Old Lady whose folly induced her to sit in a holly;
Whereon, by a thorn, her dress being torn,
She quickly became melancholy.

There was an Old Person of Ischia, whose conduct grew friskier and friskier;
He danced hornpipes and jigs, and ate thousands of figs,
That lively Old Person of Ischia.

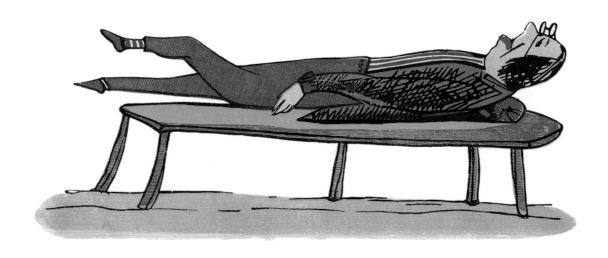

There was an Old Man of Moldavia, who had the most curious behaviour;
For while he was able, he slept on a table,
That funny Old Man of Moldavia.

There was an Old Man of Peru, who never knew what he should do;
So he tore off his hair, and behaved like a bear,
That intrinsic Old Man of Peru.

There was a Young Lady of Parma, whose conduct grew calmer and calmer;
When they said "Are you dumb?" she merely said "Hum!"
That provoking Young Lady of Parma.

There was an Old Person of Cheadle, was put in the stocks by the Beadle;
For stealing some pigs, some coats, and some wigs,
That horrible Person of Cheadle.

There was an Old Man of the Wrekin, whose shoes made a horrible creaking;
But they said, "Tell us whether your shoes are of leather,
Or of what, you Old Man of the Wrekin?"

There was an Old Man of Bohemia, whose daughter was christened Euphemia;
But one day, to his grief, she married a thief,
Which grieved that Old Man of Bohemia.

There was an Old Person of Nice, whose associates were usually Geese;
They walked out together, in all sorts of weather,
That affable Person of Nice!

There was a Young Lady of Bute, who played on a silver-gilt flute;
She played several jigs to her Uncle's white Pigs:
That amusing Young Lady of Bute.

There was a Young Lady of Turkey, who wept when the weather was murky;
When the day turned out fine, she ceased to repine,
That capricious Young Lady of Turkey.

There was an Old Person of Chili, whose conduct was painful and silly;
He sat on the stairs, eating apples and pears,
That imprudent Old Person of Chili.

There was an Old Man who said, "Well! will *nobody* answer this bell?
I've pulled day and night, till my hair has grown white,
But nobody answers this bell!"

There was an Old man with a flute — a "sarpint" ran into his boot!
But he played day and night, till the "sarpint" took flight,
And avoided that Man with a flute.

There was a Young Lady of Welling, whose praise all the world was a-telling;
She played on the harp, and caught several Carp,
That accomplished Young Lady of Welling.

There was an Old Man of Madras, who rode on a cream-coloured Ass;
But the length of its ears so promoted his fears,
That it killed that Old Man of Madras.

There was an Old Man of Quebec — a beetle ran over his neck;
But he cried, "With a needle I'll slay you, O beadle!"
That angry Old Man of Quebec.

There was an Old Person of Leeds, whose head was infested with beads;
She sat on a stool, and ate gooseberry-fool,
Which agreed with that Person of Leeds.

There was an Old Man of Berlin, whose form was uncommonly thin;
Till he once, by mistake, was mixed up in a cake,
So they baked that Old Man of Berlin.

There was an Old Man of Messina, whose daughter was named Opsibeena;
She wore a small Wig, and rode out on a Pig,
To the perfect delight of Messina.

There was an Old Man in a boat, who said, "I'm afloat! I'm afloat!"
When they said, "No, you ain't!" he was ready to faint,
That unhappy Old Man in a boat.

There was an Old Man of the North, who fell into a basin of broth;
But a laudable Cook fished him out with a hook,
Which saved that Old Man of the North.

There was an Old Person of Philœ, whose conduct was scroobious and wily;
He rushed up a Palm when the weather was calm,
And observed all the ruins of Philœ.

There was an Old Person of Ewell, who chiefly subsisted on gruel;
But to make it more nice, he inserted some Mice,
Which refreshed that Old Person of Ewell.

There was an Old Man of Dundee, who frequented the top of a tree;
When disturbed by the Crows, he abruptly arose,
And exclaimed, "I'll return to Dundee!"

There was an Old Person of Troy, whose drink was warm brandy and soy;
Which he took with a spoon, by the light of the moon,
In sight of the city of Troy.

There was an Old Person of Burton, whose answers were rather uncertain;
When they said, "How d'ye do? he replied "Who are you?"
That distressing Old Person of Burton.

There was an Old Person of Sparta, who had twenty-five sons and one "darter";
He fed them on Snails, and weighed them in scales,
That wonderful Person of Sparta.

There was an Old Man in a casement, who held up his hands in amazement;
When they said, "Sir, you'll fall!" he replied, "Not at all!"
That incipient Old Man in a casement.

There was an Old Man with a beard, who said, "It is just as I feared! —
Two Owls and a Hen, four Larks and a Wren,
Have all built their nests in my beard!"

There was a Young Lady of Poole, whose soup was excessively cool;
So she put it to boil by the aid of some oil,
That ingenious Young Lady of Poole.

There was a Young Lady of Clare, who was madly pursued by a Bear;
When she found she was tired, she abruptly expired,
That unfortunate Lady of Clare.

There was an Old Person of Rimini, who said, "Gracious! Goodness! O Gimini!"
When they said, "Please be still!" she ran down a Hill,
And was never more heard of at Rimini.

There was a Young Person of Crete, whose toilette was far from complete;
She dressed in a sack, spickle-speckled with black,
That ombliferous Person of Crete.

There was an Old Person of Chester, whom several small children did pester;
They threw some large stones, which broke most of his bones,
And displeased that Old Person of Chester.

There was a Young Lady whose chin resembled the point of a pin;
So she had it made sharp, and purchased a harp,
And played several tunes with her chin.

There was an Old Person of Gretna, who rushed down the crater of Etna;
When they said, "Is it hot?" he replied, "No, it's not!"
That mendacious Old Person of Gretna.

There was an Old Man of Columbia, who was thirsty, and called out for some beer;
But they brought it quite hot, in a small copper pot,
Which disgusted that man of Columbia.

There was an Old Man of Cape Horn, who wished he had never been born;
So he sat on a chair till he died of despair,
That dolorous Old Man of Cape Horn.

There was an Old Man of Aôsta, who possessed a large Cow, but he lost her;
But they said, "Don't you see she has rushed up a tree?
You invidious Old Man of Aôsta!"

There was an Old Man on whose nose most birds of the air could repose;
But they all flew away at the closing of day,
Which relieved that Old Man and his nose.

There was a Young Girl of Majorca, whose Aunt was a very fast walker;
She walked seventy miles, and leaped fifteen stiles,
Which astonished that Girl of Majorca.

There was an Old Man of Marseilles, whose daughters wore bottle-green veils;
They caught several Fish, which they put in a dish,
And sent to their Pa at Marseilles.

There was an Old Person of Dover, who rushed through a field of blue clover;
But some very large Bees stung his nose and his knees,
So he very soon went back to Dover.

# Index of First Lines

There was an Old Man in a casement,  106

There was an Old Man in a pew,  31

There was an Old Man in a tree,  8

There was an Old Man of Aôsta,  117

There was an Old Man of Apulia,  13

There was an Old Man of Berlin,  96

There was an Old Man of Bohemia,  85

There was an Old Man of Calcutta,  64

There was an Old Man of Cape Horn,  116

There was an Old Man of Coblenz,  19

There was an Old Man of Columbia,  115

There was an Old Man of Corfu,  12

There was an Old Man of Dundee,  102

There was an Old Man of El Hums,  22

There was an Old Man of Kamschatka,  35

There was an Old Man of Kilkenny,  36

There was an Old Man of Leghorn,  26

There was an Old Man of Madras,  93

There was an Old Man of Marseilles,  120

There was an Old Man of Melrose,  48

There was an Old Man of Messina,  97

There was an Old Man of Moldavia,  80

There was an Old Man of Nepaul,  34

There was an Old Man of Peru,  23

There was an Old Man of Peru,  81

There was an Old Man of Port Grigor,  76
There was an Old Man of Quebec—  94
There was an Old Man of th' Abruzzi,  55
There was an Old Man of the Cape,  43
There was an Old Man of the coast,  20
There was an Old Man of the Dee,  47
There was an Old Man of the East,  75
There was an Old Man of the Hague,  7
There was an Old Man of the Isles,  32
There was an Old Man of the Nile,  57
There was an Old Man of the North,  99
There was an Old Man of the South,  60
There was an Old Man of the West,  40
There was an Old Man of the West,  61
There was an Old Man of the Wrekin,  84
There was an Old Man of Vesuvius,  70
There was an Old Man of Vienna,  59
There was an Old Man of Whitehaven,  45

There was an Old Man on a hill,  15
There was an Old Man on whose nose  118
There was an Old Man who said, "How  62
There was an Old Man who said, "Hush!  25
There was an Old Man who said, "Well!  90
There was an Old Man who supposed  29
There was an Old Man with a beard,  41
There was an Old Man with a beard,  107
There was an Old Man with a gong,  50
There was an Old Man with a nose,  73
There was an Old Man with a poker,  69
There was an Old Man with an Owl,  71
There was an Old Man with a flute—  91
There was an Old Person of Anerley,  67
There was an Old Person of Bangor,  44
There was an Old Person of Bar,  30
There was an Old Person of Basing,  53
There was an Old Person of Buda,  39

# THE HARE AND THE TORTOISE
## and other fables

People have been telling stories about talking animals for centuries. The fables written by Aesop and those attributed to him, are comical, cheeky stories that mock at human behaviour, stories about animals that fight and argue and trick one another. Each fable ends with a moral that is just as apt today as it was in Aesop's Ancient Greece.

We all know the famous fables, such as The Hare and the Tortoise and The Lion and the Mouse. Children and adults alike will delight in these retellings of those and more than 100 other fables. The simple, easy-to-read text and the more than 100 colourful and comical illustrations make this a book to be enjoyed over and over again.

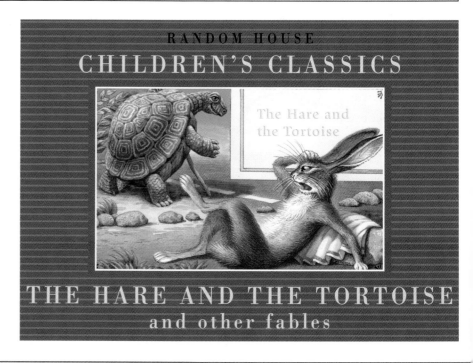

RANDOM HOUSE

CHILDREN'S CLASSICS

The Hare and the Tortoise

THE HARE AND THE TORTOISE
and other fables

# Also available in
## *The Children's Classics* series:

### *Alice in Wonderland*

Lewis Carroll's fantastic story about a little girl who disappears down a rabbit-hole and finds adventure, has been enjoyed by countless children since it was first published in 1865. Years later, Carroll decided to rewrite the story for younger children, to truly engage them in the words and pictures; he published it under the title *The Nursery 'Alice'*. We have used this version here, and combined it with delightful colour illustrations that bring this favourite classic to life.

### *Brer Rabbit Stories*

Brer Rabbit is the main character in the first ever collection of African American fables, collected by Joel Chandler Harris and published in 1880 under the title *Uncle Remus, his songs and his sayings; the folk-lore of the old plantation*. This charming trickster-hero gets into all sorts of trouble with his neighbours, Brer Fox, Brer Wolf, and many others; but every time he manages to escape the terrible fate that awaits him. These cleverly written and funny stories will thrill young children time and time again. The delightful colour illustrations bring all the characters to life, and the unusual language style means these stories are especially good to read aloud, in fact they are best read aloud.

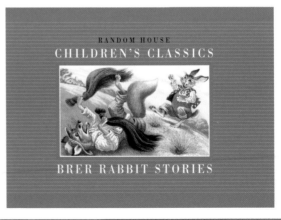

*The End*